CHAMBERS

GUI

LETTER WRITING

edited by
Kay Cullen

CHAMBERS

CHAMBERS
An imprint of Chambers Harrap Publishers Ltd
7 Hopetoun Crescent
Edinburgh EH7 4AY

www.chambers.co.uk

Reprinted 2002

A CIP catalogue record for this book is available from the British Library.

ISBN 0550 14130 8

The British National Corpus is a collaborative initiative carried out by Oxford University Press, Longman, Chambers Harrap, Oxford University Computing Services, Lancaster University s Unit for Computer Research in the English Language, and the British Library. The project received funding from the UK department of Trade and Industry and the Science and Engineering Research Council, and was supported by additional research grants from the British Academy and the British Library.

Series editor
Penny Hands

Typeset by Chambers Harrap Publishers Ltd
Printed and bound in Great Britain by
Cox & Wyman Ltd, Reading, Berkshire

Contents

Introduction

Nowadays people tend to write fewer personal letters – indeed a fair number of people would rather use any other method of communication than be obliged to put pen to paper! The telephone is convenient and immediate, but a letter is sometimes more appropriate and is often better appreciated than a quick phone call. To get a personal letter, whether it is a love letter, a thank-you letter, a letter of condolence, or simply a chatty one full of news, can be a cheering and heart-warming experience. Letters can be kept and reread again and again. They give an insight into the lives and personalities of those that have gone before us, and are important sources for biographers and historians. The first contact between job applicants and employers is almost invariably by letter, and it is always advisable to make an offer or a complaint, issue a formal warning, or confirm a booking, in writing.

Aside from the telephone, technological advances in the past couple of decades have produced some important developments in communication between businesses, educational institutions and private individuals. Fax and e-mail, for example, are so rapid and efficient that they can make contact by letter seem rather slow and laborious, particularly in business contexts and across national and international borders. However, as long as only a relatively small proportion of private individuals and smaller businesses make use of these high-tech alternatives, the traditional postal service and the telephone will continue to be the principal means by which we get in touch with each other.

This book is designed to help anyone who wants to develop their letter-writing skills. The first few chapters discuss writing materials, and give general guidance on layout, grammar and punctuation. Later chapters deal with broad subject areas, such as employment, business correspondence, complaints, and travel. In these later chapters there are many sample letters designed to help you make a start when you sit down to write to a prospective employer, complain about goods or services, or inquire about accommodation. It is perhaps worth pointing out that the sample letters are intended as a guide only, and should not be copied exactly. Although they contain many standard phrases that can be put to good use in specific contexts, what you write should, in general, be in your own voice and not in borrowed or formulaic language.

A good dictionary such as *The Chambers Dictionary* or *Chambers 21st Century Dictionary* is an essential tool for writers, especially if you have doubts about any aspect of spelling, meaning, or how a word is used in context. A thesaurus is another useful addition to your bookshelf, listing alternatives when you want to avoid repetition or well-worn expressions.

We hope this book will help you to communicate effectively and productively, and enable you to develop confidence in your letter-writing abilities.

Other guides in the same series include *Guide to Common Errors*, *Guide to Effective Grammar* and *Guide to Punctuation*.

1

Writing materials

When you are writing any letter, it is advisable to give some thought to the materials you use. The overall appearance is almost as important as the content. A neat, well-laid-out letter will not only make a good impression, but is a courtesy to the person you are writing to. This is important for letters generally, and for job applications and other formal letters in particular. A letter scrawled in blotchy green ink on grubby or cheap lined paper is likely to be treated much less seriously than one that is written or typed neatly on decent quality paper. Also, the act of writing can be made more pleasurable when you use good quality paper that won't crease or tear easily and will take ink without smudging or blotching. Unless you are corresponding with a close friend or relative, use dark blue or black ink. Avoid thick marker pens, coloured ink (other than blue or black) and pencil. If typing your letter on a typewriter, make sure the ribbon or ink cartridge in your machine will produce clear and even print.

Paper

Most of the paper we buy for writing, printing and photocopying is supplied in standard 'A' sizes. One of the advantages of this international standard for paper sizes – from the paper manufacturers' as well as their customers' point of view – is that each A size is half the area of the previous one, in a descending scale from A0 to A7. Thus, an A2 sheet folded and cut in half will produce two A3 sheets, an A3 sheet will produce two A4 sheets, and so on. A note of caution here: if you are folding and cutting paper, it is advisable to use a guillotine, which will give a straight cut edge. Ragged or uneven edges will detract from the overall appearance of your letter.

A0: 841 × 1189 mm
A1: 594 × 841 mm
A2: 420 × 594 mm
A3: 297 × 420 mm
A4: 210 × 297 mm
A5: 148 × 210 mm
A6: 105 × 148 mm
A7: 74 × 105 mm

A4 is the most popular size for business correspondence these days. A5 is also widely used, especially for shorter business letters and memos, and personal letters. Most office filing systems are designed to take A4 sheets, so it makes sense to stick to this size for correspondence that it likely to be kept for future reference.

Choose the paper size that best suits the sort of letter you are going to write. If you are writing a short note or just a couple of lines of acknowledgement, for example, use a smaller sheet size. While the text of your letter should not look cramped, neither should it float about in acres of white space! This is both wasteful and unnecessary.

For personal and less formal letters, it is perfectly acceptable to write on both sides of the sheet. If your handwritten letter stretches to more than three sides, it is a good idea to number the second and subsequent sheets.

Business and official letters should be typed or written on one side only, using continuation sheets for the second and subsequent pages.

Paper types and weights

The general advice is: use the best quality, thickest paper you can afford.

Bond

A good quality paper that will not tear or crease easily, recommended for all types of letter and for continuation sheets.

Bank

A flimsy paper that is fine for drafts, carbon copies and file copies, but because it is more transparent and will tear easily, is not recommended for the letter itself.

Airmail

A thin paper whose light weight keeps down the cost of postage for letters sent by air.

Should the paper be plain or fancy, white or coloured, lined or unlined? The best advice is to stick to plain white or cream for business, official and more formal types of personal correspondence. Notepaper with a deckle edge (a rough or wavy edge in imitation of handmade paper), in bright or fluorescent colours, with fancy scrolls printed along the edges, or with pictures of fluffy bunnies gambolling across the top of the sheet, should be reserved for letters to family members or your most intimate friends (who, it is hoped, will share your taste and be suitably appreciative).

Personalized notepaper with your name and address should, ideally, be printed by a professional printer. Be careful of using pre-printed adhesive-backed address labels or of attempting to produce a fancy design on your word-processor. Both are, of course, less costly alternatives to the professionally-produced version, but there is a certain amount of snobbery associated with personalizing notepaper and, if your aim is to impress people with your smart stationery, it is probably worth doing it properly.

Unlined paper should always be used for typed correspondence and is also recommended for handwritten letters. If you find it difficult to write by hand in evenly-spaced horizontal lines, use a guide sheet ruled up with heavy black lines under the sheet you are writing on. Pads of writing paper sold in high-street stationers often include such a guide sheet.

Envelopes

For most letters, especially social ones, the envelope should match the paper used for the letter itself. Brown envelopes are really only appropriate for business letters (invoicing, payment of bills, etc) – brown paper is cheaper and so helps to keep costs down. Manila or padded envelopes may be used when extra strength or protection is required, for example when sending multiple sheets.

Envelope sizes and types

Envelopes are available in a wide variety of sizes. Choose an envelope size that allows you to insert the letter comfortably into the envelope, with the minimum of folds.

If you don't want to fold an A4 sheet, use a C4 size envelope. The C5 size will take an A4 sheet folded once, or an A5 sheet unfolded; the C6 size will take an A5 sheet folded once, or an A6 sheet unfolded.

Many business letters are sent in envelopes measuring 100mm by 220mm. These take an A4 sheet folded neatly twice over. When using this size of envelope, make sure the folds in the A4 sheet are made with the corners of the sheet precisely aligned – there isn't much of a space allowance, and refolding or an extra small fold will detract from the appearance of your letter.

The Royal Mail uses electronic sorting for letters up to a certain weight and within a certain size range. The envelope sizes which come within this range are known as POP (Post Office Preferred) sizes: envelopes should be no smaller than 90mm by 140mm and no larger than 120mm by 235mm; and, with contents, should weigh no more than 60 grams.

Window and aperture envelopes are sometimes used for business letters. A window envelope has a square or oblong panel cut out and covered with a transparent material through which the address can be viewed. In an aperture envelope, there is no transparent protective covering over the cut-out section. The letter inside must be folded and inserted correctly so that the address appears in the correct position under the window or aperture.

Airmail envelopes are specially printed sheets that function as both writing paper and envelope, with the postage pre-paid. Guide marks are printed on the sheet indicating how it should be folded before sealing.

2

Layout

Having given some thought to the type and size of paper, the next (and equally important) aspect of letter-writing to consider is the setting out of your letter.

Setting out your letter

It is important to achieve a good balance between the size of the sheet of paper and what is to be written on it. It will detract from the overall appearance if the first sheet is closely spaced, and only one or two short lines go over on to the second sheet. Try to space the letter more generously, so that more text appears on the second sheet.

Remember that a draft will make it easier to refine and correct the content before you begin to write or type your letter. The final letter, whether it is handwritten or typed, should be free of corrections and errors.

> ⓘ If you use a word processor – especially one of the newer word-processing programs available for use on personal computers, and incorporating some of the features of desk-top publishing – much of the setting-out and formatting can be done automatically by the machine. Word-processing is discussed in greater detail in Chapter 16.

The text of your letter should be positioned on the page with appropriate spacing. The print or handwriting should be neither too cramped nor too widely spaced. Use a two line space between paragraphs or individual lines if this will improve the general appearance. If the letter is short, the text should not be pushed up to the top of the sheet with a large area left blank at the bottom – leave some space at the top to balance that at the bottom of the sheet.

Blocked and indented styles

Letters can be presented in one of two styles: blocked style or indented style. Nowadays, the majority of business letters and most other typed or word-processed letters are in blocked style. The indented style is a more traditional format and is now rarely used for business letters. However, some people still prefer the indented style for both formal and informal letters, especially those that are handwritten.

In blocked style, the sender's address is written or typed on the right hand side of the first sheet with the first letter of each new line of the address coming immediately below the first letter or number on the line above. The recipient's address, the opening greeting, the heading, the text of the letter, the complimentary close and the sender's name are all aligned to the left margin of the sheet. Note that at least one line space must be inserted between each of these elements as well as between each paragraph of the main text.

In indented style, the sender's address is typed or written on the right hand side of the sheet but with the second and subsequent lines of the address beginning one or two characters to the right of the first letter of the preceding line. If the recipient's address is included it is aligned to the left of the sheet as for blocked style. The salutation is aligned to the left hand margin, any heading following the salutation is centred above the main text of the letter, and the first line of each paragraph of the main text is indented. Line spaces between the paragraphs of the main text are optional in indented style. The indent does the work of distinguishing the paragraphs but some formal typed letters in indented style also include a line space between the paragraphs so that the text is evenly distributed on the page. The complimentary close can be indented from the left margin, centred under the main text or (in some formal typed letters) placed near the right hand margin of the sheet. Note also that punctuation is used in the indented style where it is omitted in blocked style – there are usually commas at the line ends of the addresses and after the saluation and complimentary close.

(See also section on punctuation in Chapter 3

Layout of a formal letter (blocked style)

25 Julian Way
Broomloan
GLASGOW
G99 0ZZ

31st December 1999

The Manager
Glasgow and Scottish Bank plc
300 Great Scott Street
GLASGOW
G09 1YY

Dear Sir

Account No. XXXXXXX J D Haddington

This is to confirm my telephone call to the branch this morning asking that you stop payment of a cheque issued by me in favour of Breakneck Builders Ltd. It is cheque number 145678, written for the sum of £895.50, and dated 21st December 1999.

Breakneck Builders have informed me that they have not received the cheque, and I have therefore concluded that it has been lost in the post.

I would be grateful if you would confirm that the original cheque has been stopped, so that I may issue a new one.

Yours faithfully

James D Haddington

James D Haddington

Layout of an informal letter (in indented style)

25 Laburnum Road,
ABERDEEN
AB6 6FW

Saturday, 17th April

Dear Anne,

I was delighted to get your long letter yesterday. I hadn't expected to hear from you so soon after your removal, as I'd been thinking you'd be much too busy arranging your new home and settling the children into their new school.

I'm so glad that all your lovely furniture survived the move intact, and that nothing is missing. I hope you have nice neighbours and that Tom and Chloe make friends quickly. Of course they will miss their old school friends for a while but they have so many hobbies and interests I'm sure they will soon belong to as many clubs as they did here, and that all their spare time will be occupied with interesting activities.

We all miss you, and I especially miss our daily chats. We must arrange to visit each other later in the year, perhaps in the school holidays. I'm sure you will want to come back to Scotland for the New Year, and of course you must stay with us.

I'm sorry to hear that your mother isn't very well. I'm sending her a 'get well' card, which I hope will cheer her up.

I'll phone you sometime next week.

Love,

Deirdre

Layout of a business/official letter (blocked style)

PHOTOTECH plc
4-14 Ploughshare Road
NORWICH N00 5RR
Tel: 01793 68809 Fax: 01793 68810

Our Ref: SNA-T/KE/MMP
Your Ref: PB/HC
Date: 10th July 1999

J M Butterworth Ltd
25 Middlefarm Road
DIDCOT
OXON
OX12 6JJ

Attention: Mr P Brandon

Dear Sir

Thank you for your letter of 3rd July asking for a copy of our product catalogue.

As requested, I also enclose our current price list. This gives details of the discounts offered for bulk orders and our terms and conditions for payment.

When you have had an opportunity to study the catalogue, a meeting can be arranged with one of our representatives, who will be able to discuss your requirements in more detail.

If, in the meantime, you have any general queries, please do not hesitate to get in touch with us.

Yours faithfully

Kenneth Evans

Kenneth Evans
Marketing Manager

cc RMcD, LDW

Encs

A business/official letter

An official letter or a business letter is always written on the firm's or organization's headed notepaper. The name, address, telephone number, etc printed at the top of the page is known as the letterhead. If the firm or organization has a logo this will printed as part of the letterhead.

Addressing the envelope

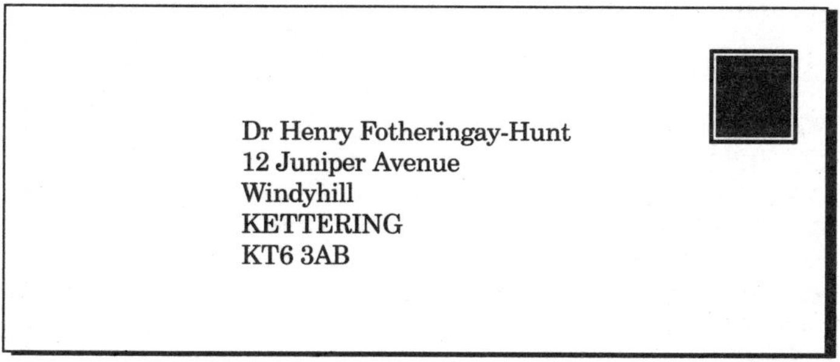

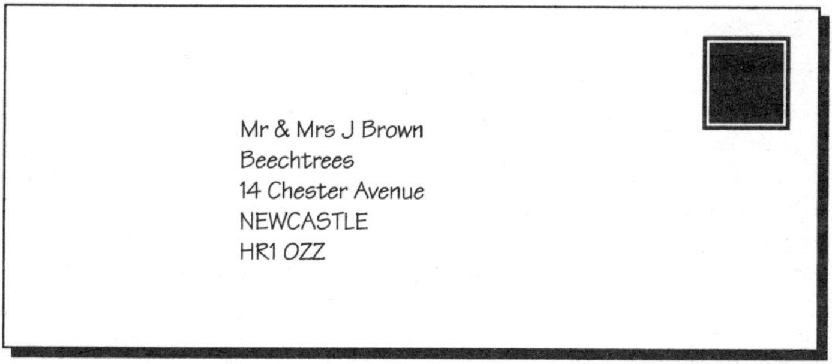

The address should be aligned with the longer sides of the envelope. It should be positioned slightly to the left of the mid point between the two shortest sides, with the first line of the address about two thirds of the way down from the top edge of the envelope. This allows plenty of room for the stamp and postmark.

The address on the envelope should include: the name and title of the recipient; the house/building name or street number + street name; locality name (area of town or city); post town (in block capitals); country name or region (this is not required when the post town is a large town or city); and post code (always in block capitals with a space between the two parts of the code). Each element should be on a new line. Note that the post office prefers that no punctuation be used in the name and address on the envelope. This is so that the letter can be scanned and sorted electronically.

Sender's address on the envelope

Many businesses use address labels with their own name and address printed along the top or bottom edge, or use envelopes printed with their logo and address. This helps the post office if the letter or package has to be returned to the sender for any reason. If you are concerned that your letter may not reach its destination, or that the post office will not be able to deliver it, you should write or print your own name and address on the back of the envelope, making it clear that you are the sender. This is standard practice in most EU countries and in North America.

Stamps

Postage stamps should be affixed to the top right hand corner of the letter above and to the right of the address. The stamp or stamps should be stuck on the right way round, with the top edge aligned to the top edge of the envelope. It isn't necessary to emulate the overly-particular character in a well-known British TV comedy series, who uses a ruler to align the stamp perfectly – postal sorting offices use laser technology to scan, locate and frank the stamp on the envelope and their machines are quite capable of dealing with slight misalignments. However, for the sake of a neat appearance, don't stick the stamp on any old way!

If your letter is heavier than the maximum weight allowed for a standard first or second class stamp, make sure you affix stamps of the correct value.

Abbreviated forms on the envelope

In addresses, there are several conventional abbreviations used in customary titles (eg *Dr*, *Prof*, *The Rev*, *The Right Hon*) and in the street names (eg *St*, *Ave*, *Blvd*, *Rd*). There should be no full stops in these abbreviations when written on the envelope.

3

Grammar and punctuation

The odd instance of bad grammar or poor punctuation may go unnoticed in a personal letter. However, in formal and business letters your aim should be to get your message across clearly and unambiguously, and the structure of your sentences should reflect this aim.

Grammar and style

It is a good idea to vary the length of sentences within paragraphs. This will give your letter a more natural flow. Short paragraphs (each dealing with a single central point or idea) are preferable to long ones, which may cause the reader to skip over important details.

Here are some grammar rules that you might want to keep in mind as you write:

- Use active rather than passive verbs and try to keep to the same tense.
- Verbs should agree with their subject in person (*I go*, *he goes*) and number (*She goes*, *they go*).
- Where a verb like *be*, *seem*, *appear* is used to link a singular subject with a plural complement, the verb should be in the singular: *Our main concern <u>is</u> our expenses*. When the subject is plural and the complement is singular the verb should be in the plural: *Our expenses <u>are</u> our main worry.*
- Avoid double negatives: *I never knew no greater joy.*
- Avoid double comparatives: *It was much more quicker than I expected*. And, double superlatives: *It is at the most furthest point away from the centre.*
- It is advisable to avoid splitting too many infinitives (ie inserting

a word between *to* and a following verb), though this is not strictly ungrammatical: *He started to gradually realise his mistake.*

- The words *even* and *only* should be placed as closely as possible to the word or words they are intended to emphasize.
- Take care not to use a dangling participle: *Driving along a country road last week, a tree fell on our car.* This wording suggests that the tree was driving.
- A word or words may be wrongly omitted (the omission of words in sentence construction is known as ellipsis). Avoid, in particular, the omission of the preposition that always accompanies a particular verb: *I was dreaming* (of) *and hoping for a long break*.

Punctuation

Letters are nowadays usually typed in blocked style with 'open punctuation': that is, with the minimum punctuation required for clarity. This applies in the addresses, the main text of the letter and other elements in the letter, such as the salutation, heading and complimentary close.

Addresses on the letter

In blocked style no punctuation is required in the sender's address or the recipient's address. There should be no commas after the house number, no inverted commas around a house name. Nor should there be any full stops after abbreviations of any kind.

Mandalay
14 Plumtree Rd
GREENSWARD
Kent GW3 4JP

Dr A J Thorne
45 Greenview Ave
JOHNSVILLE
Lancs JV37 6MH

When writing or typing letters in indented style, many people prefer to insert a comma after the house number and at the end of each line of both the 'sloping' sender's address and the recipient's address. However, commas are not obligatory in indented style and may equally correctly be left out. As in blocked style, there should be no inverted commas around a house name. Full stops may be used after abbreviations of customary titles (eg *Dr, Mrs, Mr*) and street names (eg *Rd, St, Ave*), or, equally correctly, may be omitted. A full stop is often used (though may also be omitted) after the type of abbreviation that does not include the first and last letter of the full form (eg *Prof., The Rev., Lancs., Bucks.*). Initialisms (eg *UK, USA*) should have no full stops.

Mandalay
14, Plum Rd,
GREENSWARD,
Kent GW3 4JP

Dr A J Thorne,
45 Greenview Gardens,
JOHNSVILLE,
Lancs. JV37 6MH

Address on the envelope

Whether the letter itself is typed or written in blocked or indented style, there should be no punctuation in the address on the envelope. The postcode should be on a separate line with no full stops or underlining.

Dr A J Thorne
45 Greenview Gardens
JOHNSVILLE
Lancs
JV37 6MH

Punctuation in the date

No punctuation is required in the date when it is written in the order day (in figures), followed by month (written out in full), followed by year (in figures):

29 November 1999

If you choose to include the name of the day as well as its number, it is usual to insert a comma between the name and number:

Sunday, 29 November 1999

Other styles used in writing dates do have punctuation of one sort or another. There may be hyphens between the elements, as in:

29-Nov-99

Or, slashes between the elements, as in:

29/11/99
29/11/1999

Or, stops between one or more of the elements, as in:

29.11.99
29 Nov. 99

> ⓘ When writing dates using figures for all the elements (as in *12/7/99*) remember that the order of the day and month is reversed in the US and in countries that have adopted the US system. In the US *12/7/99* means *7 December 1999*, while in Britain it means *12 July 1999*.

The punctuation of other elements in a letter

In blocked style there is no comma after the salutation or the complimentary close. In indented style a comma after these elements is usual in both typed and handwritten letters, though is not obligatory.

In business and official letters, a colon is used in various conventional elements that are outside the main text of the letter. These include the reference line or lines, the attention line, and in a subject heading made up of two parts.

Our reference: LW03/KMC

Your reference: KB/MM

Attention: Mr K Barnes
For the Attention of: Dr Isabel Stewart

Expenses: new claim forms
Account number: X00000

Punctuation in the main text of the letter

The punctuation of the main text of your letter should follow the rules that apply to any piece of writing. These rules can be summarized as follows:

Full sentences

Begin each sentence with a capital letter and end it with a full stop, a question mark or an exclamation mark. A full stop is used at the end of a sentence that is a statement, a question mark at the end of a sentence that is a question, and an exclamation mark at the end of an interjection, an exclamation or a command.

Apostrophe

An apostrophe is used:

- to create the possessive form of nouns: *the man's hat, Niall's pals, the children's names.*
- in contracted forms at the point where one letter is, or several letters are, omitted: *they've, he's, we're, hadn't.*

> ⓘ Note that *it's* (with an apostrophe) is the short form of *it is*. The possessive form, eg *its back bumper,* has no apostrophe.

Comma

A comma is used:

- to separate items in a list: *the cat, the dog and the guinea pig*
- between two co-ordinated main clauses linked by 'but' or 'or': *I would like to visit you, but I can't get any time off work.*
- after a subordinate clause that comes before the main clause in a sentence: *When it did start to rain, it didn't stop for a week.*
- after an adverb that links the sentence to the previous one: *I was very tired. However, we had to keep walking.*

- before or after a 'commenting' word or phrase at the end (or beginning) of a sentence: *Regrettably, I shall not be able to attend the conference in Cairo.*

A pair of commas is used:

- to enclose the type of relative clause that adds information. Commas are only required where the sentence would still make sense if the relative clause were removed: *The bus, which must have been at least fifty years old, groaned and creaked under the weight of so many passengers.*
- to enclose a commenting word or phrase in the middle of a sentence: *Then he took off all his clothes, I kid you not, and sprinted off down the high street.*

> ⓘ Remember to include the second enclosing comma. It is a common error to omit it, especially if the clause to be enclosed is a long one.

Colon

A colon is used to indicate that what follows explains, expands on or completes the part that has gone before. What follows the colon may be a complete sentence, a list or even a single word: *There's a new film on at the local cinema: Hamlet, I think.*

Semicolon

A semicolon is used instead of a word like 'and' or 'but' to separate two clauses of equal importance: *He made another dive for the ball; he missed again.*

A semicolon is also used to separate groups of items in a list, often one where individual items are separated by commas: *He made a wonderful curry with the leftover chicken, a few mushrooms and some chopped tomatoes; saffron rice with coconut, sultanas and chopped parsley; and a sweet dish using honey and nuts.*

Brackets or parentheses

Brackets are used to enclose an extra piece of information inserted into a sentence and which defines, illustrates, explains or comments: *The plane (a 747) was unable to land.*

4

Spelling and vocabulary

This chapter includes some guidance on spelling and appropriate vocabulary.

Spelling

If you are unsure of the spelling of a word, always check it first in a dictionary. Bad spelling will not only distract the reader from the content of your letter, but will give the clear message that you have not taken the trouble to get it right. If you are having your letter typed by someone else, always check it for typographical errors before you sign it. A word processor with a spell-checking facility is helpful, but remember that spell-checkers are not infallible and are unlikely to recognize proper names or technical terms. Nor do they help if you have used the wrong word, but have spelt it properly.

It is important, for courtesy's sake, to spell the name of the recipient correctly, and to get their job title right. If necessary, check the spelling of their name in the telephone book, or make a quick telephone call to the company they work for to make sure all the details you have are correct.

Spelling checklists

Words that have the endings *-able* or *-ible* are so often misspelled that it is worth including a list of the commonest ones, for easy reference. Note that some words can be spelt with either ending.

accessible	capable	compatible
advisable	changeable	contemptible
agreeable	collapsible	creditable
amicable	collectable/collectible	culpable
applicable	communicable	despicable

detachable
detectable/detectible
detestable
edible
eligible
enviable
fashionable
fallible
feasible
flexible
forcible
formidable
foreseeable
gullible
horrible
hospitable
indelible
indefensible
indestructible
inevitable
inexcusable
inexhaustible
inflammable
inflexible
intolerable
irrepressible
irresistible
knowledgeable
lamentable
legible
memorable
negligible
noticeable
payable
peaceable
perceptible
permissible
plausible
pliable
portable
possible
predictable
preferable
preventable/
preventible
probable
reliable
reprehensible
respectable
responsible
reversible
saleable
sensible
sociable
susceptible
tangible
terrible
transferable
unforgettable
unforgivable
unmistakable
unstoppable
usable/useable
variable
viable
visible
vulnerable

Here are some more words that are frequently misspelled or whose spellings can be confused.

abandoned
absence (noun)
absent (verb)
accept
accidentally
accommodation
accuracy
accurate
achieve
acknowledge
acquaintance
acquire
across
address
advice (noun)
advise (verb)
affect (verb)/effect
(noun)
amateur
answer
apology
apologize
apparently
appearance
appreciate
argument
assess
assist
assistance
assistant
attach
autumn
awful
awfully
baggage
beautiful
beginner
beginning
behaviour
believe
breadth
Britain
brochure
business
calendar
cancel
cancelled
cancelling

cancellation
career
careful
carefully
catalogue
category
colleague
commit
commitment
committed
committing
comparative
concede
connection
convenience
correspondence
courteous
deceive
December
decide
decision
decisive
definite
definitely
deliberate
dependant (noun)
dependent
(adjective)
describe
develop
developed
developing
difference
disappear
disappoint
disapprove
discrepancy
dispatch or despatch
dissatisfied
eighth
embarrass
embarrassment
envelope
equipped

especially
etc (et cetera)
exaggeration
excellent
exciting
exhibition
experience
extraordinary
extremely
favourite
February
financial
finish
foreign
foreigner
forty
friend
fulfil
gauge
government
grateful
grief
grieve
guarantee
guard
guess
guidance
guide
happened
happening
height
honorary
honourable
humorous
humour
hygiene
hygienic
immediately
inaccurate
incidentally
independent
install
installation
instalment

intelligence
interrupt
journey
knowledge
language
leisure
liaise
liaison
licence (noun)
license (verb)
maintenance
manoeuvre
marriage
medicine
message
messenger
millennium
mortgage
necessary
neither
niece
ninth
nuisance
occasionally
occur
occurred
occurring
omit
omission
opportunity
opposite
ordinary
passenger
permanent
permit
permitted
permitting
personal
personnel
persuade
piece
planning
possess
possibility

practice (noun)
practise (verb)
prefer
preferred
preparation
principal (adjective)
principle (noun)
privilege
probably
pronounce
pronunciation
pursue
receipt
receive
recommend
reference
refer
referred
referring
referral
repetition
resign
satisfactory
schedule
scheme
sentence
separate
sign
similar
sincerely
skilful
stopped
stopping
subtle
succeed
suddenness
sympathy
technical
temporary
thorough
through
travel
travelled
travelling
Tuesday
twelfth
unfortunately
unnecessary
vehicle
Wednesday
whole
wholly

Vocabulary

Check that all the words you have used mean what you intend them to mean. Think carefully whether they will be understood by the reader, and whether they are suitable for the type of letter you are writing (not too informal and 'slangy', nor on the other hand too formal and pretentious). Avoid, if you can, jargon, clichés and repetition.

Writers of business letters, in particular, often fall into the trap of using formulaic or highfalutin expressions so as to create what they imagine is a suitably detached and business-like tone. However, many of these expressions are nowadays regarded as relics of a bygone age or just plain pompous. It is always better to err on the side of simplicity and clarity – don't use twenty long words where three or four short ones will do.

Try to get your message across using plain English: most everyday words are as appropriate in formal contexts as in informal ones. Ask yourself if it is necessary to use, for example, *purchase* instead of *buy*, *proceed* instead of *go*, *cease* instead of *stop*, *endeavour* instead of *try*, or *commence* instead of *start*. More often than not, the more familiar word will do the job just as well.

Try to avoid using combinations of words and phrases that are tautological: that is, where a second word or phrase is used that repeats the meaning of one used earlier in the same sentence, as in the rather extreme example: *We must insist that immediate payment of all outstanding sums is made forthwith.*

Here are some examples of well-worn expressions that should be avoided if possible (or even at all costs!), with comments in brackets:

- Assuring you of our best attention at all times.
  [unnecessary – this is taken as read, at least if you want to get or keep my custom!]
- a copy of same
  [drop the 'of same' or recast the sentence]
- at this moment in time
  [a cliché – 'now' is shorter and simpler]
- at your earliest convenience
  ['as soon as possible' *or* 'as soon as is convenient' is simpler]
- consequent upon
  [old-fashioned/legalese – 'after' is clearer and simpler]
- due to the fact that...
  [unnecessarily wordy – 'because' will do the job]
- enclosed herewith
  ['enclosed' *or* 'I enclose' is quite sufficient]
- inst., prox., ult.
  [Latin abbreviations used to refer to the current, next or previous month: now very old-fashioned – instead, name the month]
- in early course
  [pompous as well as being too vague to serve any useful purpose: be more specific or use 'soon' *or* 'as soon as possible' if you want to keep your options open]
- in the course of
  ['during' is more straightforward]
- Re your letter of...
  ['I/We refer to your letter of...' is preferable]
- yours to hand
  [This is only used by writers who are caught in a time warp around the middle of the nineteenth century!]

5

Beginnings, endings and correct forms of address

The opening greeting or salutation

In business letters, the usual opening greeting should begin with 'Dear'. Conventionally, a letter addressed to a company or organization (but without specifying a particular person or job title) should begin 'Dear Sirs'. If the letter is addressed to, for example, 'The Human Resources Manager', or marked for someone's attention, the greeting should be 'Dear Sir' or 'Dear Madam'.

For formal letters addressed to an individual, the 'Dear' is followed by the customary title (eg Mr, Miss, Mrs, Ms) and name of that individual (eg Dear Mr Jones, Dear Dr Smith).

Correct forms of address for people of rank and title are dealt with later in this chapter.

The opening greeting for informal letters can be in any form you think appropriate, 'Dear Peter', 'My dear Anne', 'My dearest Bunny', 'Darling Bill'.

The complimentary close

For business and formal letters, use the form of the complimentary close that matches the opening greeting.

Thus, if your letter begins 'Dear Sirs', 'Dear Sir' or 'Dear Madam', the complimentary close should be 'Yours faithfully'.

> ⓘ Never use 'Yours very faithfully'.

If the person is named in the opening greeting, the complimentary close should be 'Yours sincerely' or (slightly more friendly in tone) 'Yours very sincerely'.

For a business letter and other formal letters where you are well known to your correspondent, the complimentary close used may be less formal and might include 'Best wishes' before the 'Yours sincerely'.

For informal letters, the complimentary close can, like the opening, be in any form you think appropriate, 'Love', 'Much love', 'With all my love', 'Yours ever', etc.

In the United States, the 'Yours sincerely' and 'Yours faithfully' formulae are routinely reversed, as 'Sincerely yours' (or simply 'Sincerely'), and 'Faithfully yours'. Similarly, the rarely used 'Yours respectfully' (only appropriate in certain types of business letter) would be 'Respectfully yours' or 'Respectfully' in the US.

Correct forms of address

You may have occasion to write to someone who holds an official title or rank, such as a member of the clergy or a peer of the realm. The correct forms to use in the address and opening greeting are shown below.

Archbishop (Anglican)

- Address on letter and envelope: The Most Reverend the Archbishop of —
- Open letter with: My Lord Archbishop
- Close letter with: Yours faithfully

Archbishop (of Canterbury and York)

- Address on letter and envelope: The Most Reverend and Rt Hon The Lord Archbishop of —
- Open letter with: My Lord Archbishop
- Close letter with: Yours faithfully

Archbishop (Catholic)

- Address on letter and envelope: His Grace the Archbishop of —
- Open letter with: My Lord Archbishop *or* (less formally) Dear Archbishop
- Close letter with: Yours faithfully

Baron

- Address on letter and envelope: The Right Hon Lord [surname]
- Open letter with: My Lord *or* (less formally) Dear Lord [surname]

Baroness (wife of baron)

- Address on letter and envelope: The Right Hon Lady [surname]
- Open letter with: Dear Madam *or* (less formally) Dear Lady [surname]

Baroness (in own right)

- Address on letter and envelope: The Right Hon Lady [surname] *or* The Right Hon the Baroness of [surname]
- Open letter with: Dear Madam *or* (less formally) Dear Lady [surname]

Baronet

- Address on letter and envelope: Sir [forename] [surname], Bt
- Open letter with: Dear Sir *or* (less formally) Dear Sir [forename]

Bishop (Anglican)

- Address on letter and envelope: The Right Reverend The Lord Bishop of —
- Open letter with: My Lord Bishop *or* My Lord
- Close letter with: Yours faithfully

Bishop (Roman Catholic)

- Address on letter and envelope: His Lordship the Bishop of —
- Open letter with: My Lord
- Close letter with: Yours faithfully

Cardinal

- Address on letter and envelope: His Eminence Cardinal [surname]
- Open letter with: Your Eminence
- Close letter with: Yours faithfully

Chief Rabbi

- Address on letter and envelope: The Very Reverend the Chief Rabbi
- Open letter with: Dear Chief Rabbi *or* Dear Sir
- Close letter with: Yours faithfully

Christian Clergy (Anglican and Protestant Churches)

- Address on letter and envelope: The Reverend [forename] [surname]
- Open letter with: Dear Sir/Madam *or* Dear Mr/Mrs [surname]

Christian Clergy (Roman Catholic)

- Address on letter and envelope: The Reverend [forename] [surname] (If a member of a religious order, the initials of the order should follow the name)
- Open letter with: Dear Reverend Father

Councillor

- Address on letter and envelope: (for a man) Councillor [forename] [surname]; (for a woman) Councillor Mrs/Miss [forename] [surname]
- Open letter with: Dear Councillor [surname]; Dear Councillor Mrs/Miss [surname] *or* Dear Mr/Mrs/Miss

Countess

- Address on letter and envelope: The Right Hon the Countess of —
- Open letter with: Madam *or* (less formally) Dear Lady —

Dame

- Address on letter and envelope: Dame [forename] [surname] (followed by letters of the order)
- Open letter with: Dear Madam *or* (less formally) Dear Dame [forename]

Doctor (of medicine)

- Address on letter and envelope: Doctor *or* Dr [forename] [surname]
- Open letter with: Dear Doctor *or* Dr [surname]
- See also **Surgeon**

Doctorate, holder of

- Address on letter and envelope: the initials DD, LLD, MD, MusD, etc may be placed after the ordinary form of address
- Open letter with: Dear Sir/Madam *or* Dear Dr [surname]

Duchess

- Address on letter and envelope: Her Grace the Duchess of —
- Open letter with: Dear Madam *or* (less formally) Dear Duchess

Duke

- Address on letter and envelope: His Grace the Duke of —
- Open letter with: My Lord Duke *or* (less formally) Dear Duke

Earl

- Address on letter and envelope: His Right Hon the Earl of —
- Open letter with: My Lord *or* (less formally) Dear Lord —

Governor (US)

- Address on letter and envelope: The Honorable [forename] [surname] Governor of [state]
- Open letter with: Dear Governor [surname]

Judge (High Court)

- Address on letter and envelope: The Hon Mr/Mrs Justice [surname] (note that *Mrs* is used even to an unmarried woman) *or* Sir/Dame [forename] [surname]
- Open letter with: Dear Sir/Madam *or* (less formally) Dear Judge *or* Dear Sir/Dame [forename] [surname]

Judge (Circuit)

- Address on letter and envelope: His/Her Honour Judge [surname]
- Open letter with: Dear Sir/Madam *or* (less formally) Dear Judge

Knight

- Address on letter and envelope: Sir [forename] [surname] followed by the initials of the order, eg KCB (of the Bath), KCMG (of St Michael and St George), KG (of the Garter), KT (of the Thistle)
- Open letter with: Dear Sir *or* according to person's rank

Life Peer

- Address on letter and envelope: The Right Hon the Lord [surname]
- Open letter with: Dear Lord [surname]
  (note that the full title, eg *Lord Holden of Hazeldean*, should not be used on letters. Use only *Lord Holden*)

Life Peeress

- Address on letter and envelope: The Right Hon the Baroness [surname]
- Open letter with: Dear Baroness [surname] *or* Baroness
  (as with a life peer use only the title and surname in the address)

Mayor

UK and Ireland

- Address on letter and envelope: The Worshipful the Mayor of [town or city] *or* (for some cities and towns) The Right Worshipful the Mayor of —
- Open letter with: Mr Mayor (even if a woman, though some women prefer Madam Mayor) *or* Dear Mr/Madam Mayor

> ⓘ Note that the Lord Mayors of London, York, Belfast, Cardiff and Dublin are addressed as *The Right Hon the Lord Mayor of —* with the salutation *My Lord Mayor* or *Dear Lord Mayor*; for other Lord Mayors use *The Right Worshipful the Lord Mayor of —* in the address and *My Lord Mayor* for the salutation.

United States

- Address: The Honorable (full name), Mayor of (city)
- Begin letter: Dear Sir/Madam *or* Dear Mr/Madam Mayor

Member of Parliament

- Address on letter and envelope: the usual form of address, followed by MP
- Open letter with: Dear [title] [surname]

Officers (serving in the Armed Forces)

- Address on letter and envelope: The professional rank precedes any other rank or title.
- Open letter with: Dear [rank] [surname]

Officers (retired)

- Naval officers above the rank of Lieutenant, army officers above the rank of Captain, and airforce officers above the rank of Flight Lieutenant may continue to use and be addressed by their armed forces rank after being placed on the retired list

Pope

- Address on letter and envelope: His Holiness the Pope
- Open letter with: Your Holiness *or* Most Holy Father
- Close letter with: (for Roman Catholics) I have the honour to be, your Holiness's most humble (*or* devoted and obedient) child; (non-Catholics) I have the honour to be (*or* remain), Your Holiness's obedient servant

President of the United States

- Address on letter and envelope: The President
- Open letter with: Sir/Madam *or* Dear Mr/Madam President

Prime Minister

- Address on letter and envelope: The Right Hon [forename] [surname], MP (unless holding another rank that takes precedence)
- Open letter with: Dear Sir/Madam *or* (less formally) Dear Prime Minister (or address according to any other rank held that takes precedence)

Prince

- Address on letter and envelope: (if a duke) His Royal Highness the Duke of —; (if the son of the sovereign, but not a duke) His Highness, the Prince [forename]; (otherwise) His Royal Highness Prince [forename]
- Open letter with: Sir
- Close letter with: I have the honour to be (*or* remain), Sir, Your Royal Highness's most humble and obedient servant

> ⓘ Note that for royalty, it is more usual to address any correspondence to a private secretary, equerry, or lady-in-waiting.

Princess

- Address on letter and envelope: (if a duchess) Her Royal Highness the Duchess of —; (if the daughter of the sovereign, but not a duchess) Her Royal Highness, the Princess [forename]; (if a princess by marriage) HRH Princess [husband's forename] of —; (otherwise) Her Royal Highness Princess [forename]
- Open letter with: Madam
- Close letter with: I have the honour to be (*or* remain), Madam, Your Royal Highness's most humble and obedient servant

Professor

- Address on letter and envelope: Professor [forename] [surname]
- Open letter with: Dear Sir/Madam

Queen

- Address on letter and envelope: Her Majesty the Queen

- Open letter with: Madam, with my humble duty
- Close letter with: I have the honour to be (*or* remain), Madam, Your Majesty's most humble and obedient servant

> ⓘ Note that for royalty, it is more usual to address any correspondence to a private secretary, equerry, or lady-in-waiting. If writing to the Queen's private secretary the address on the letter and envelope should read *The Private Secretary to Her Majesty the Queen* and the letter should begin *Dear Sir.*

Representative (US Federal)

- Address on letter and envelope: The Honorable [forename] [surname]
- Open letter with: Sir/Madam *or* Dear Congressman/Congresswoman [surname]

Senator (Federal)

- Address on letter and envelope: The Honorable [forename] [surname]
- Open letter with: Sir/Madam *or* Dear Senator [surname]

Surgeon

- Address on letter and envelope: Mr/Mrs/Miss [forename] [surname]
- Open letter with: Dear Mr/Mrs/Ms [surname]

> ⓘ In England and Wales, obstetricians and gynaecologists are addressed as for a surgeon; in Scotland, Ireland and elsewhere as for a doctor of medicine.

Viscount

- Address on letter and envelope: The Right Hon the Viscount —
- Open letter with: My Lord *or* (less formally) Dear Lord —

Viscountess

- Address on letter and envelope: The Right Hon the Viscountess —
- Open letter with: Madam *or* (less formally) Lady —

6

Writing letters to other countries

Writing to European (Union) countries

A word of warning for people writing from Britain or Ireland to continental European countries: unless you are fluent in the language of the country you are writing to (or are practising the language by writing to a pen pal who will in turn practise their English when writing to you), you should write in English (keeping your message as short and simple as possible). Alternatively, you can have your letter translated into the appropriate language by a professional translator.

For most EU countries (except France and Greece), the street number is written on the envelope after the street name, and the postal code comes before (and on the same line as) the post district or town. For France and Greece, the street number is written before the street name, and the postal code comes before (and on the same line as) the post district or town.

When sending letters to the United Kingdom, you should specify the country: England, Scotland, Wales or Northern Ireland. 'UK' can be added after the country name.

Do not address letters simply 'Ireland': write instead 'The Republic of Ireland' (not 'Eire') or 'Northern Ireland'.

Addressing mail to the USA

The following guidelines are those issued by the United States postal authorities to ensure that addresses on envelopes can be processed by the postal service's automated equipment

The address should be entirely in capital letters.

First line:	ADDRESSEE'S NAME
Second line:	NUMBER, STREET, APARTMENT NUMBER or POST OFFICE BOX NUMBER
Third line:	CITY, STATE, ZIP CODE (POSTAL CODE)
Fourth line:	UNITED STATES OF AMERICA

Below is a list of the official postal abbreviations of American states, to be used when addressing envelopes bound for America.

Alabama	AL	Montana	MT
Alaska	AK	Nebraska	NE
Arizona	AZ	Nevada	NV
Arkansas	AR	New Hampshire	NH
California	CA	New Jersey	NJ
Colorado	CO	New Mexico	NM
Connecticut	CT	New York	NY
Delaware	DE	North Carolina	NC
Florida	FL	North Dakota	ND
Georgia	GA	Ohio	OH
Hawaii	HI	Oklahoma	OK
Idaho	ID	Oregon	OR
Illinois	IL	Pennsylvania	PA
Indiana	IN	Rhode Island	RI
Iowa	IA	South Carolina	SC
Kansas	KS	South Dakota	SD
Kentucky	KY	Tennessee	TN
Louisiana	LA	Texas	TX
Maine	ME	Utah	UT
Maryland	MD	Vermont	VT
Massachusetts	MA	Virginia	VA
Michigan	MI	Washington	WA
Minnesota	MN	West Virginia	WV
Mississippi	MS	Wisconsin	WI
Missouri	MO	Wyoming	WY

7

Formal and informal style

Formal letters

Formal letters are written to, for example, your local councillor, your member of parliament, or a prospective employer.

The formal letters written by private individuals on social and personal matters are similar in layout to the business letters sent out by commercial companies and other organizations (see Chapter 2 for the basic layout of formal and business letters, and Chapter 8 for business letters). However, business letters are only one type of formal letter, and they tend to be more heavily structured, with abbreviated reference lines, date lines, etc and various other conventional forms that are not required in other types of formal letter.

Here are some points to remember when you are writing any formal letter that is not a business letter:

- You must, of course, include your name and address, the date, and the name and address of the person or organization you are writing to.
- Begin your letter with the appropriate opening greeting and end it with a corresponding complimentary close.
- Give your letter a heading. This will help the recipient to see at a glance what your letter is about. The heading should follow the opening greeting and be typed or written on a new line with at least one line space above and below it. The heading in a typed or handwritten letter is usually underlined or typed/printed entirely in capital letters to make it stand out. If you are using a word processor you have the option of using bold type or type of a larger size for the heading.
- For non-business formal letters, avoid using the conventional abbreviations found in business letters, such as 'Enc' for 'enclos-

ure' and 'cc' for 'copied to'. The person you are writing to may not be familiar with these abbreviations. It is therefore preferable to write out such points within the letter itself, ie 'I enclose ...', and 'I am sending a copy of this letter to ...'.

Organizing and structuring the content of a formal letter

Always be polite and succinct. Rambling explanations with too much information in one paragraph will make it difficult for your reader to extract the point you are trying to make.

It is a good idea to structure your letter so that there is a short introductory paragraph, which may be used to acknowledge any previous letter you have received and to state the subject of your letter. This can be followed by a longer paragraph or series of paragraphs developing or expanding the various points you want to make in a logical sequence and providing relevant details where required.

End with a short final paragraph (the conclusion).

For examples of formal letters on various subjects see Chapters 8-14.

Informal letters

When writing to friends and relatives, you are, of course, free to write in any way you see fit, using a relaxed conversational style. The letter may be handwritten, typed or written on a word processor. People whose handwriting is very difficult to read should consider using a typewriter or word processor. If you are writing to, for example, an elderly relative whose eyesight isn't very good, use black or dark blue ink on white paper to give good contrast. Using a word processor allows you to increase the size of type – this will also help a reader with poor eyesight.

Letter to a close friend

written in informal/conversational language

short forms and contractions

236 Montgomery Road
BATH
Avon
BA14 7DU

6th June 1999

Dear Beth,

Hi! How are you? I'm sorry I haven't been in touch for so long but I seem to have been really busy recently. After the exams Mum said I could decorate my bedroom, so that's what I've been doing in my spare time.

How were your exams? Mine were pretty tough. Though I did lots of studying I think I might have failed Biology. English Lit and History were okay though, and I'm hoping for B's at least. We should get our results soon, so I'll let you know how I get on.

Where are you off to on holiday this summer? We're going to Cornwall for a fortnight as usual, but we haven't been able to get the cottage we usually rent in St Agnes. It will be strange going somewhere else, though Ben, of course, doesn't care where he stays as long as he can get a bit of surfing in. Brothers!

Thanks for the photos. The ones of us going up Snowdon came out really well. My legs get sore again when I think about the walk, but it was great fun.

Write soon and tell me all your news, and say hi to your Mum and Dad from me.

Lots of love
Claire
X X X

new paragraph for new subject

8

Business letters

This chapter looks at business correspondence: the types of letters that businesses and other organizations send out to, and receive from, external sources. Business letters are, in the main, formal in tone and should be brief, to the point, accurate and polite. They are always typed and are nowadays usually in blocked style (see Chapter 2) with the minimum of punctuation. There should, for example, be no full stops in abbreviations.

Nearly all commercial companies and large organizations use pre-printed headed stationery for their letters, invoices and order forms. Customarily, a letter from a business, or an organization such as the Inland Revenue, will have an internal reference, which usually includes the initials of the person who has signed it. Reference lines (internal and external) and date lines may be pre-printed on the firm's or organization's stationery with the letter-head. The firm's internal reference (usually beginning with 'Our reference:' or 'Our ref:') should always be quoted in any reply to the letter using the formula 'Your reference:' or 'Your ref:'.

A letter or order from the outside should be acknowledged within a matter of two or three days of the date it was received, so that the sender knows that the matter is being dealt with. An acknowledgement may be in the form of a short letter or a post-card. It should state when the letter/order was received and confirm that the matter is being dealt with.

Letter/card of acknowledgement for order

Automotive Direct
6 Netherdale Road
CHICAGO
IL 1053

July 23 1999
Our ref: T13607-99RT
Your ref: P126/GW

G Wendell, Esq
NewPark Motor Supplies Ltd
300 Depot Road
CHICAGO
IL 1176

Dear Customer

This is to acknowledge receipt of your order no 5698 dated July 20 1999.

The order is receiving our immediate attention and will be dispatched to you by July 30 1999.

I hope we may continue to receive your valued custom.

Paul Ryder

Paul Ryder
Despatch Officer

Letter placing an order

Watts Office Supplies
88 Prince Edward Road
BRISTOL
MR4 0ZZ

Customer Service Manager
Middlemarch Diaries
6 Consort Way
TUNBRIDGE WELLS
Kent
TN1 6BG

5th October 2000

Dear Sir

2001 Diary Order

I refer to your letter of 30th September enclosing your catalogue of diaries for 2001. I would like to place an order for some of the products advertised.

I enclose a completed order form. I assume that the amount payable will be subject to the usual trade discount. Please advise if this is not the case. Please also advise of the preferred method of payment.

I look forward to receiving your confirmation of my order, and would be obliged if you would advise me in advance of the planned delivery date, so that I can reorganize my stock accordingly.

Since I want to display next year's diary's from early November, I would be grateful if you would give this matter your urgent attention.

Yours faithfully

Charlie Watts

C Watts
Chief Buyer

cc B Jones

Letter from supplier requesting reference

Maygold plc
456-460 Queens Road
CARDIFF
CF22 0ZZ

Our ref: NAS/10/MM
Your ref: D889/HW

Mr R Fleck
NorthEast Paper Products Ltd
78 Ship Road
NEWCASTLE
NH1 0ZZ

25th July 1999

Dear Mr Fleck

Thank you for your order of 20th July 1999, which is receiving our prompt attention.

As you are a new customer, we would be grateful if you would supply us with a standard banker's reference for our records. Alternatively we would be pleased to receive your remittance before your order is dispatched.

Yours sincerely

Marjorie Mead

Marjorie Mead
Accounts

Reply to invoice

Watts Office Supplies
88 Prince Edward Road
BRISTOL
MR4 0ZZ

D George
KELPACK Ltd
44-48 Westbrae Street
BIRMINGHAM
BB1 0JJ

23rd October 2000

Dear Mr George

Payment of Invoice no BD767

Thank you for the prompt delivery of our order no. C00145.

Please find enclosed a cheque for £327.50 in payment of your invoice no. BD767 of 30 September 2000.

Yours sincerely

David Wallace

D Wallace
Buying Assistant

Response to a complaint about goods damaged in transit

KELPACK Ltd
44-48 Westbrae Street
BIRMINGHAM
BB1 0JJ

Mr J Ritchie
Carlton Cartons Ltd
44 Merryfleet Way
PLYMOUTH
PL3 0ZZ

14th June 1999

Dear Mr Ritchie

I refer to your letter dated 11th June 1999 which arrived this morning with the consignment of damaged boxes you advised you would be returning to us.

I apologize most sincerely for the inconvenience this has caused you and have dispatched this morning a replacement consignment of boxes which will reach you on 17th June.

Once more please accept my sincere apologies.

Yours sincerely

Theo Smith

Theo Smith
Customer Services Manager

Sales promotion letter

MADDOCK PUBLISHING Ltd
Southbrae Industrial Estate
LONDON
W67 OPP

30th July 2000

Simon Software Inc
2 Landmark Square
ATLANTA
Georgia 30303

Dear Sir/Madam

Publishing Opportunities in Europe

We are an established publisher of European trade and business journals with high visibility throughout the Economic Community, Central and Eastern Europe. Currently we are offering special advertising rates and benefits to new customers.

This is an excellent opportunity for your company to increase its share of the IT market in the dynamic European market place.

Please find enclosed two copies of our journals, with our compliments. If you wish to pursue our offer (attached) or require any further information, please contact our enquiry line on Freefone 0800 3765.

I look forward to hearing from you and to our possible future partnership.

Yours faithfully,

J. C. Mitchison

J. C. Mitchison
Sales Director

Memos

Memos (or memorandums) are used for sending messages to employees or colleagues within a business or organization, though not necessarily in the same building. Much of the information that was formerly disseminated within an organization via memos is now carried on computer networks, which link departments, individuals, and remote branches within the same organization.

Most paper memos are in the following format:

TO:
FROM:
CC:
DATE:
SUBJECT:

Some abbreviations and acronyms found in business correspondence

a/c	account
ad val.	ad valorem (according to the value)
AGM	annual general meeting
APR	annual percentage rate
approx.	approximately
asap	as soon as possible
av.	average
b/d	banker's draft (banking)
bc.	blind copy (of a memo, letter)
bcc.	blind carbon copy
be, BE	bill of exchange
c.	circa (approximately)

C&F	cost and freight
cc	carbon copy (copies to)
CEO	Chief Executive Officer
chq	cheque
C/N	consignment note; cover note; credit note
c/o	care of; carried over; cash order
Co	company, county
COD	cash on delivery
contd, cont'd	continued
CV	curriculum vitae
DD	direct debit
del.	delivery; delivered
Dir	Director
D/N	debit note
E&OE	errors and omissions excepted
eg, e.g.	for example (Latin *exempli gratia*)
enc(s)	enclosure(s)
FAO, fao	for the attention of
HM	His/Her Majesty's
ie, i.e.	in other words (Latin *id est*)
Inc., Incorp	incorporated
incl.	included, including
infm., info	information
inst	of this month
L/C	letter of credit
Ltd	limited company
mgr.	manager
NB	note well (Latin *nota bene*)
NIS	not in stock
O/D	overdraft
ono	or nearest offer
OOS	out of stock
p.a.	per annum (each year)
p&p	postage and packing
PAYE	pay as you earn
PLC	public limited company
p.o.	postal order
pp	on behalf of (Latin *post procurationem*)
pps	additional postscript

Pres.	president
ps	postscript
PTO	please turn over
rcd	received
re	with reference to
rec.	recommend
Ref	reference
req(d)	required
retd	retired
sae	stamped addressed envelope
sase	self-addressed stamped envelope
SO	standing order
SOR	sale or return
viz	namely
VP	Vice-president

9

Complaints and responses

Letters of complaint

Avoid writing a letter of complaint in a white heat of rage or indignation. While it may relieve your feelings, the result is likely to be rather incoherent and, in the long run, will probably be less effective than a letter that is polite but firm and sticks to the facts. This applies equally when you are writing to complain about something that has offended you and when you are complaining about goods and services.

Complaints about goods and services

When making a complaint about goods and services, first muster all the relevant facts, check that they are accurate, and then set them out coolly and clearly in a logical sequence. In claims for a refund or compensation, have a clear goal in mind and state what you want by way of redress. Knowing your rights as a consumer is always an advantage. You can, if necessary, quote the relevant legislation in your correspondence.

Give your letter a heading. If you are complaining about faulty goods, include in the heading any details that will help to identify the item in question, such as the order number or the model or product number. For other services, quote any reference number printed on the invoice or agreement.

Keep copies of all the letters you send and a note of the time and date of any phone calls made. If you are making a claim of any sort, documentary evidence may be needed in the event that the claim is contested.

If there is no named individual to whom you can address your complaint, direct your letter in the first instance to the Customer Services Manager or, for smaller companies and family businesses, the owner or managing director (he or she is the person who will be concerned about the firm's image and therefore most likely to take prompt action).

Make sure you make a claim for a refund or compensation within any time limit defined under the relevant Act. Also set a time limit (of a reasonable period) for when you expect to receive a response from the company or organization, and state this in your letter. If you do not receive, at the very least, an acknowledgement within the time limit you have set, write again.

It is a good idea to send your letter by recorded delivery. A signature is required for the letter when it is delivered, and the other party will not therefore be able to claim they have not received it.

Useful phrases

- I wish to draw your attention to...
- I wish to complain about...
- I wish to complain, strongly, about...
- I am extremely concerned that...
- When the goods arrived I found the following defects/damage...
- I experienced the following problems...
- The service was unsatisfactory in the following ways...
- Under the terms of your guarantee...
- It was implied in the contract between us...
- I look forward to receiving, within the next 14 days, a reasonable offer/your written proposal...

Responding to a complaint

Large commercial organizations receive sackloads of letters every year from people who have put pen to paper – often on the spur of the moment – to complain. No matter how abusive the writer may be, no matter how wild their views are, a polite and measured response is the only appropriate one.

Commercial organizations should always respond to customer complaints about goods and services, and in the shortest possible time. Entering into a dialogue with the customer at an early stage is much more likely to achieve a satisfactory result for both parties.

See also sample letters in Chapter 8 Business Letters.

Letter complaining about faulty goods

7 Morningside Drive
EDINBURGH
EH9 4AY

The Customer Services Manager
Whitegoods plc
Lowburn Industrial Park
EDINBURGH
EH39 1GG

4th August 1999

Dear Sir or Madam

Kleanquik Automatic Washing Machine. Model number 9337.

I purchased the above model of washing machine from your Wallace Street store on 15th July 1999. It was delivered and installed by your service engineer on 19th July 1999.

On 30th July 1999, only eleven days after the machine was installed, it developed a serious fault, causing water to flood out of the front of the machine. I immediately telephoned the store and informed them of this. They advised me that an engineer would call on Tuesday 2nd August at 11 a.m. I waited at home for the whole of 2nd August, but no engineer called. I have telephoned the store repeatedly and each time was informed that someone would call me back. No one did.

I must therefore insist that you inform me in writing of your proposals to remedy this situation by providing me in the first instance with a firm date and time when your engineer will call. While I am prepared to give you a further opportunity to honour your guarantee and the terms of the service agreement that exists between us, I reserve my right to claim compensation for the inconvenience already caused to me and to reject the goods as unsatisfactory under the terms of the Sale of Goods Act 1979.

Yours faithfully
Jane Pearson
Jane Pearson (Mrs)

Letter complaining about defective workmanship

6 Eastrow Cottages
NEWPORT
NP3 4DD

RECORDED DELIVERY

John Carpenter & Sons
38 Cardiff Road
NEWPORT
NP1 9FF

4th August 1999

Dear Sirs

I wish to complain about one of the new locks your firm fitted on my front door on 2nd August 1999, after my home had been broken into the previous evening. I paid you £197.50 inclusive of VAT for the work. I enclose a copy of your receipted invoice for that amount.

The defective lock has two loose screws on the interior side of the door, which were obviously not anchored sufficiently firmly to the wood. As a result the lock is no longer properly aligned with the door jamb, making it difficult to turn the key.

I am offering you the opportunity to carry out the necessary work to rectify the defect. Please confirm that you will do so as a matter of urgency, at no additional cost to me. I must emphasize that time is of the essence. If the necessary work is not carried out within the next 7 days, I shall have no alternative but to employ another firm, and am legally entitled to recover the costs incurred from you.

Yours sincerely

A.S. Swinton

A.S. Swinton (Mrs)

Letter complaining about unsatisfactory service

20 Selsdon Way
YORK
YK15 7DS

The Customer Services Manager
East Coast Mainline
King's Cross Station
LONDON
N00 3ZZ

23rd August 1999

Dear Sir or Madam

I am writing to complain about the inconvenience caused to me last week by your company's inadequate performance.

I was booked to travel on the 08:00 train from York to London on 19th August. This was due to arrive in London at 11:00. I had been assured, when I booked my ticket, that this would give me plenty of time to change platforms and catch the 11:35 train to Bedford, where I had an important appointment. However, we arrived in London at 11:47, more than three-quarters of a hour late. I therefore missed my connection.

I am more than disappointed with the service I received and feel I am entitled to compensation which reflects adequately the inconvenience suffered.

I look forward to receiving your response within the next 14 days.

Yours faithfully

B. Anderson

B. Anderson

Letter responding to a complaint

John Carpenter & Sons
38 Cardiff Road
NEWPORT
NP1 9FF

Mrs A S Swinton
6 Eastrow Cottages
NEWPORT
NP3 4DD

6th August 1999

Dear Mrs Swinton

Thank you for your letter of 4th August in which you advised that one of the new locks which were fitted at your property recently by one of our joiners is not working satisfactorily.

I am very concerned that if there is any question of faulty workmanship or a defect with the lock itself that this should be put right at the earliest opportunity, and therefore suggest that I call round on Friday morning at 9 a.m. so that I can examine the lock personally and have any necessary repairs carried out immediately. You may be assured that if the fault lies with us that any repair or replacement will be carried out at no additional cost to you.

Please telephone me directly if the suggested arrangement is not to your convenience.

Yours faithfully

Robert Carpenter

Robert Carpenter
Director

10

Employment

This chapter gives guidance on letters to prospective employers, how to present your CV (or, in American English, 'résumé') and a letter of resignation.

Job applications

Letters of application should be written with great care. A well-written letter could lead to an interview, whereas a badly written one will almost certainly lead to your application being rejected.

The person or organization to which you send your application is likely to have many others to read and consider, and it is therefore important that your application conveys the necessary information neatly and succinctly. Unless the advertisement for the post you are applying for specifies that the application should be in your own handwriting, the letter should be typed or written on a word processor. You should, of course, sign the letter in your own hand.

Letter of application (without CV/résumé)

Your letter of application should include the following details:

- your home address and telephone number;
- a heading stating clearly which post you are applying for;
- where you heard about the post or saw it advertised;
- your age, education and training;
- your present job (if you have one) and any previous employment;
- any other experience, qualifications or interests relevant to the post;
- the names and addresses of two referees, or a reference to any letters of recommendation you are enclosing.

Flat 1
64 Plockenden Road
Islington
LONDON
N1 0ZZ

Tel: 01234 567 8910

Alexander Maxwell
Personnel Manager
Kingsway Shopping Centre
Walford
LONDON
N2 0ZZ

12th October 1999

Dear Mr Maxwell

Shopping Centre Supervisor

I am writing in response to your advertisement in this week's 'Retail News' for a shopping centre supervisor.

I am twenty years old, and have just completed a year's training in business studies at Thames College. I left school last summer with 5 GCSEs and two A Levels (English and Maths). During holidays and at weekends, I have worked in a clothes shop as a sales assistant, and also in a newsagent's, where I was often left in charge. I am keen to follow a career in the retail industry, and think this post will give me the responsibility I am looking for.

Should you consider me suitable for the post, I can provide the names of three referees.

I look forward to hearing from you, and should you wish to, please do not hesitate to contact me at home at the above number.

Yours sincerely

Jonathan Lee

Jonathan Lee

CV/résumé and covering letter

It is now common for job advertisements to state that applicants should write, in the first instance, a brief letter enclosing their CV (curriculum vitae) or 'résumé' (in American English). Because your CV/résumé will include all your personal details and work history, it is not necessary to duplicate all this information in the letter which accompanies it. Keep in mind that the aim of the covering letter is to give only enough information to engender interest and to encourage your reader to offer you an interview.

Here are some useful points to remember when writing the covering letter.

- The covering letter should be handwritten if this is specified in the advertisement. Otherwise it may be typed or produced on a word processor.
- It should be on a single sheet of good quality white paper. Ideally, the paper used for the covering letter should be of the same size as that used for your CV/résumé.
- Remember to include your home address, telephone number, and the date.
- Take care to get the name and title of the person or organization you are writing to exactly right.
- Begin the letter with a short paragraph saying where you saw the post advertised and mentioning that you are enclosing your CV/résumé.
- The first paragraph may be followed by a single sentence or short paragraph drawing attention to qualifications or experience that you consider are particularly relevant, or giving any other reason why you believe you are a suitable candidate for the post.
- Conclude with a short paragraph offering availability for interview.
- Remember to sign a typed or word-processed letter in your own hand.

Covering letter to accompany CV/résumé

200 Bairdmore Blvd
WINNIPEG
Manitoba
R3T 5HZ

September 16 1999

Ms A Dalrymple
Chief Analyst
Longthorn Investments
490 Akron Road
VANCOUVER
British Columbia
S4J 2NP

Dear Ms Dalrymple

Financial Analyst

I should like to apply for the above post which was advertised in today's Financial Post, and I enclose my current résumé for your attention.

I am an experienced financial analyst, consultant and presenter, having worked extensively in this sector both in Toronto and New York. I am currently looking for a position which will allow me to develop my skills and experience in a small, dynamic commercial team such as Longthorn Investments. I believe that my financial and academic background would be of benefit to your strategic financial planning, and the building of partnerships with investment houses throughout North America and the Far East.

Thank you for considering this application. I look forward to discussing matters further with you at a future interview.

Sincerely yours

Robert Jones

Robert Jones
Financial Investment Analyst

Unsolicited application (with CV/résumé)

45 Forest Way
CARDIFF
CA3 0NN

Tel: 1234 567 8910

L Hamilton
Personnel Officer
Globetech (UK) Ltd
75 Enderley Street
SWANSEA
SS1 0ZZ

15th July 1999

Dear Mr Hamilton

I wish to enquire about any vacancy you may have in your Sales Department. Your customer services manager, Dewi Griffiths, who belongs to a sports club of which I am also a member, suggested I write to you. He tells me that your firm is expanding, and will therefore be recruiting new people in the very near future.

As you will see from the enclosed CV, I have a good educational background and twelve years' experience in sales, both as a sales representative and sales executive.

My present employers, Clearview International, are closing their Cardiff factory at the end of August and I am to be made redundant at that time. I am anxious not to remain without work for long, and am willing to consider any suitable post that becomes available.

Should you consider my application favourably, I should be pleased to attend an interview at any time.

Yours sincerely

William Preston

William Preston

CV/résumé (recent graduate)

STEPHEN EDWARD FORBES

Address: 81 Lincoln Walk, Stevenage, Herts SE19 2DN
Tel: 01283 456789
e-mail: sforbes@teaser.org.uk
Date of birth: 5th October 1977
Nationality: British
Marital status: single

EDUCATION

1995–1999

University of Swansea, Wales BSc Applied Mathematics (2.2)

1995

(A Levels) Maths (A), Chemistry (B), Biology (B)

1994

(GCSEs) English Language (A), Maths (A), Chemistry (A), Biology (A), Computer Studies (A), French (B), History (B).

1988–1995

Whitton Comprehensive, Bristol BS1F 8UF

WORK EXPERIENCE

October 1998

3 week placement as assistant technician with Bond Research, Swansea

Summer 1996

Waiter at Horseshoe Hotel, Swansea

SKILLS

Full, clean driving licence
Computer literate (Word for Windows, Excel, PageMaker)

INTERESTS

At school I was a Prefect and a founding member of the Drama Club. At university I was a member of the Debating Society. I also wrote articles for the Student Union newsletter. I am a keen hillwalker and enjoy competitive sailing.

Referees: available on request

CV/résumé (experienced candidate)

MARY GRANT

Address:198 Francis Avenue, Leicester LE4 9PQ
Tel: 01493-767-3336
e-mail: mgrant@USA.net
Date of birth: 6th October 1966

WORK EXPERIENCE

1992 to present
Gannet UK Ltd, Greenwich, London – Corporate Training Manager

- Delegation and implementation of training throughout corporation
- Marketing and Sales of training materials to French and UK market
- Delegate to European Training Council
- Design of new courses and presentation to new customers

1989–1992
Simon & Co plc, Leicester – Training Consultant

- Designed and managed technical training programmes
- Delivered workshops, seminars and group projects
- Organized international conferences

EDUCATION

1984–1988
M.A. in Business Studies with French
Edinburgh University, Edinburgh

1982–1984
HNC Business and Economics
Stevenson College, Edinburgh

Reply to offer to attend an interview

An offer to attend an interview should always be responded to in writing.

45 Forest Way
CARDIFF
CA3 0NN

Tel: 1234 567 8910

L Hamilton
Personnel Officer
Globetech (UK) Ltd
75 Enderley Street
SWANSEA
SS1 0ZZ

21st July 1999

Dear Mr Hamilton

Thank you very much for your letter of 20th July. I would be happy to attend an interview on 25th July at 10.30 a.m. and will bring with me the two references you request.

Yours sincerely

William Preston

William Preston

Letter of resignation

148 Kennedy Drive
SHELTON
Connecticut 0463

September 14 1999

Alison Farmer
Healthy Foods Ltd
Unit 7
Westcote Business Park
SHELTON
Connecticut 0984

Dear Mrs Farmer

As I explained to you earlier this afternoon, I have, for some time now, been concerned that I have not been given adequate resources to develop new product lines, which I believe will be essential if Healthy Foods is to maintain its current position in the market and compete effectively.

You made it clear that this would not be a priority for the foreseeable future, and I therefore think it would be best if I sought a position elsewhere. I am writing to give you one month's notice of the termination of my contract, effective from today's date.

I would be grateful if you would acknowledge this letter.

Sincerely yours

Oliver Smeaton

Oliver Smeaton

11

Travel and holidays

Making travel arrangements and booking accommodation is often done by telephone or through an agent. However, it is a good idea to confirm any telephone enquiry or booking in writing so that each party if clear about what is required or expected from the other.

When writing to enquire about accommodation it is important to include in your letter all the relevant details, as well as describing any specific requirements you may have. Similarly, if you are confirming a telephone booking in writing, all the details you have discussed and agreed with the hotel or guesthouse should be included in your letter of confirmation. The same applies when you are booking a package holiday – send a letter together with the booking form describing any special requirements you may have and ask that the tour operator confirm in writing that the holiday will conform to all your requirements.

When enquiring about or confirming accommodation include the following details:

- the number of rooms and beds; be specific about details such as en suite shower and wc, sea view, or facilities for the disabled;
- the period of time; give departure and arrival times where possible and days and dates;
- say whether it is to be bed and breakfast, half board or full board;
- ask about the price or confirm the price agreed;
- ask that your booking be confirmed in writing.

The Internet is playing an increasingly important role in providing travel information. Net users can browse travel guides and assess what is available in most parts of the world without having to wade through brochures or make repeated visits to their travel agent. In many cases it is possible to arrange your itinerary, book flights and accommodation, and arrange car rental online. As the number of sites increases, and more and more people gain access to the Net, a greater proportion of the business of getting from A to B, and arranging for a place to stay when you get there, is likely to be conducted over the Internet.

Booking a hotel room

7 Adelaide Street
BOSTON
MA 06743

June 13 1999

The Manager
Harkers Lodge
HIGH RIVER
Alberta
A4G 7MX

Dear Sir or Madam

I saw your advertisement in this month's *Country Pursuits*. My wife and I will be traveling around Alberta in August and September, and, if possible, I would like to reserve a room for three nights from September 16 to 19 inclusive. Ideally, I would prefer a room with an en suite bathroom. Since my wife has difficulty climbing stairs, we will need a room situated either on the first floor or near a lift.

I would be grateful if you could let me know if you have a suitable room free on those dates. If so, please advise me of the total price to include breakfast. It would also be very helpful to us if you would forward details of local events and interesting places to visit in your area.

I look forward to hearing from you soon.

Faithfully yours,

Alan Nixon

Alan Nixon

Confirming a holiday booking

7 Adelaide Street
BOSTON
MA 06743

June 20 1999

Mrs F McLeod
Harkers Lodge
HIGH RIVER
Alberta
A4G 7MX

Dear Mrs McLeod

This is to confirm the telephone booking I made on the evening of June 18 1999.

My wife and I require a double room on the first floor from September 16 to 19 inclusive; the room to have en suite bathroom with shower. The all-inclusive price for bed and breakfast for three nights, with dinner on the evening of September 17, will be $375.00 as agreed.

I enclose my check for $85.00 as deposit.

Sincerely yours

Alan Nixon

Alan Nixon

enc

Asking your employer for holiday entitlement

Telephone Sales Dept
Ground Floor

15 February 1999

Mr A Norris
Human Resources Manager

Dear Mr Norris

I would like to take one week of my holiday entitlement from 27th April to 1st May, two weeks in August (17th to 28th inclusive) and the remaining two weeks from 21st December to 1st January inclusive.

I hope this is suitable.

Yours sincerely

Mary Gillanders

Mary Gillanders

12

Invitations and replies

There are two types of formal invitation: a printed card and a formal letter.

Formal invitations on printed cards are always written in the third person and are traditionally printed in black. A standard card may be sent to all the prospective guests, or the cards may be personalized, with the guest's name written or printed on the card. There should be no date, opening greeting or complimentary close. The letters *RSVP* (an abbreviation of the French phrase *répondez s'il vous plaît*) mean 'Please reply'. When receiving a formal invitation in either form, if it is in the third person, you must also reply in the third person.

Printed card (standard form to all guests)

Mr and Mrs Kenneth Jones
request the pleasure of your company
at the marriage of their daughter
Elizabeth
to
Mr Edwin Forsyth

at Glasgow Cathedral
on Saturday 16th June
at 2.30 p.m.
and afterwards at the reception at
The Craigard Hotel, Glasgow

RSVP
116 Cleveden Crescent
Glasgow GG1 0ZZ

Printed card (naming individual guests)

Mr and Mrs Kenneth Jones
request the pleasure of
the company of

[name(s) of guests]
at the marriage of their daughter
Elizabeth
to
Mr Edwin Forsyth

at Glasgow Cathedral
on Saturday 16th June
at 2.30 p.m.
and afterwards at the reception at
The Craigard Hotel, Glasgow

RSVP
116 Cleveden Crescent
Glasgow GG1 0ZZ

When replying to a formal invitation, whether accepting or declining the invitation, your reply should be handwritten. Remember that if the original invitation was in the third person you should also reply in the third person. There is no need to date or sign the reply. Note also that if you are declining a formal invitation you need only state that you are unable to attend – you are not required to give a reason.

A formal invitation in the form of a letter may be in the third person, or if slightly less formal, in the first and second persons. It should, of course, include an opening greeting and a complimentary close, but otherwise the information will be the same as for the printed-card version.

Replies to informal invitations can be in the form of a short handwritten note or letter.

Courtesy demands that any invitation, whether formal or informal, be replied to as quickly as possible.

An informal invitation (to an event such as a wedding) may be (neatly) handwritten, typed or written on a word processor. If typed or printed, the names of the invited guests should be added by hand.

Informal invitation

Aunt Carol and Uncle Will

James and I hope that you will be able to come to our wedding at Breedale Church, Blacksburgh, on Saturday 20th June at 1.30 p.m. The reception is at The Horse and Hound in Breedale Road. Please let us know if you will be able to come.
Love from

Silvia

91 Victoria Road
Cirencester
Gloucestershire
GL15 4JD

Acceptance of an invitation (formal)

Mr and Mrs Armitage thank Mr and Mrs Fowler for their kind invitation to their daughter's wedding, and to the reception afterwards. They have much pleasure in accepting.

Declining an invitation (formal)

Mr and Mrs Armitage thank Mr and Mrs Fowler for their kind invitation to their daughter's wedding, and to the reception afterwards, but regret that a prior engagement prevents them from attending.

Acceptance of an invitation (informal)

4 Maitland Street
CASPER
Wyoming 0538

July 13 1999

Dear Lucy,

Thanks so much for the invitation to your barbecue. I'll be delighted to come. It will be really good to see you all again.

Do you think I'll be able to get a bus from here? I'll phone you nearer the time to arrange the details. Meanwhile, let's hope the weather stays good for the barbecue! Thanks again for the invitation.

Look forward to seeing you soon.

Love,

Maria

13

Thank-you letters

Thank-you letters should be handwritten, and in most situations it is quite appropriate to use an informal conversational style of writing.

When the thank-you letter is for a wedding, birthday, or Christmas present don't just write 'Thank you for the lovely present ...'. You should mention what the present was, as in 'Thank you for the beautiful silver serving spoons/fabulous diamond necklace/postal order for £2.50...'. This will show that you know which present has been given by which person and avoid the impression that you are dashing off a whole series of standard thank-you letters simply because this is what is expected of you. Remember that the aim should be to convey your appreciation to the individual concerned, so personalize these letters as much as possible and try to use your own words rather than formulaic expressions.

Although children nowadays often prefer to phone the people who have given them presents, and this is becoming more and more acceptable, encouraging them to write letters is no bad thing, especially when thanking older relatives who are more likely to regard a short letter as more appropriate than a phone call. Again, a letter in their own words will probably be enjoyed much more than one which has obviously been dictated by an adult.

Letters to work colleagues thanking them, for example, for a leaving gift or party should be written from your home address. The envelope should be addressed to the most senior member of staff and the letter itself to all the staff concerned.

It is obligatory to write a thank-you note when you have been to someone's house for a formal dinner, or have been to stay with them. Similarly, if a business contact or acquaintance has entertained you to lunch or a trip to the theatre, this should be acknowledged in writing with your thanks. The thank-you letter should, of course, be sent as soon after the event as possible.

Thanks for a wedding present (before the event)

The Poplars
38 Skye Road
Ayr
AH1 9XX

18th April 1999

Dear Christine and Sandy,

Thank you very much for the beautiful crystal glasses you sent us as a wedding present. They will look wonderful on our dinner table, and you must come for a meal and try them out, when we get back from France.

It is lovely that you can both come to the wedding and we are very much looking forward to seeing you on the 21st.

I don't think John and I have ever been so busy, with all the organizing to do. There always seems to be something that still needs to be attended to!

We look forward to seeing you, and many thanks again.

With love

Jenny and John

Jenny and John

Thanks for a wedding present (after the event)

Forest View
1008 White Lakes
REDMOND
Oregon 0970

April 18 1999

Dear Kristy and Max,

We are writing to thank you for the beautiful umbrella stand you bought us as a wedding present. It looks fantastic in the hall and is just the right style for the house.

It was really nice to see you at the wedding – we had a wonderful day and it all seemed to run smoothly, thanks mainly to Brett and my Mum. We had a lovely honeymoon in Hawaii and are settling in well to the new house.

You must come and see us soon, and many thanks again.

With much love,

Nancy and Brett

Nancy and Brett

Thanks for hospitality

14 Westmorland Crescent
Whitecombe
Bedfordshire
SG16 7GB

12th October 1999

Dear Anne and Nigel,

We've just got back and I wanted to write to you immediately to tell you what a great weekend we had with you. Thanks a lot for inviting us – it was a real break for us both.

I didn't realize before that you lived so close to the sea – it was really relaxing going for walks along the beach. We especially enjoyed the meal in the pub on Sunday. It was a great little place, and the beer wasn't bad either.

I do hope we can come back and visit you again soon.

Remember, you're always welcome to come and stay with us any time. We have plenty of room here, and there are some interesting places we could visit.

Thanks again for putting us up, and keep in touch!

All the best

Carol and Mike

Carol and Mike

Thanks for a dinner party

14 Westmorland Crescent
Whitecombe
Bedfordshire
SG16 7GB

12th November 1999

Dear Jon and Karen

That was a wonderful meal you gave us last night! Thank you so much.

It was lovely to see Louise and Martin again, and chat about old times.

You must all come to us next time and we'll arrange something before Christmas, before everyone goes off on holiday.

With love

Donna and Patrick

14

Sympathy and condolence

Illness: letters of sympathy

The tone and content of a letter expressing sympathy for an illness will depend very much on your relationship with the person and whether or not the illness is serious. When the condition, disease or injury is one from which the sufferer is likely to recover, the letter can be light and cheerful, even humorous. If the illness is more serious and it is known or suspected that recovery is unlikely, the approach needs to be somewhat different: misplaced optimism, detailed reference to the illness itself, or a bantering style may only cause further distress to the patient and their close relatives. An acceptable alternative in most circumstances is to send a 'Get well soon' or 'Sympathy' card (again, depending on the nature of the illness) with a short personal message.

If you do decide to send a letter, it should, preferably, be handwritten.

Sympathy to the relative of an ill person (formal)

10 Carr Avenue
Willerby
Nr Hull
HU12 7KD

14 May 1999

Dear Mrs Clitheroe

I was very sorry to hear of Mr Clitheroe's illness. Please accept my sympathies and give him my best wishes for a speedy recovery.

Yours sincerely
Agnes Wright

Sympathy to an ill person (informal)

13 Trevelyan Rise
Falmouth
Cornwall
FA5 8LC

6 March 1999

Dear Rachel

I was very sorry to hear from Marion that you have been taken ill so suddenly. Acute appendicitis is very painful and alarming. I wish I had known earlier and I would, of course, have visited you while you were in hospital. I'm very glad to hear that you are now back home and on the road to recovery. You'll need plenty of rest after your operation, but I'm sure Harry is making sure that you don't do too much too soon.

I'd like to come and visit later in the week. Let me know when would suit and if there is anything you need. I have some paperbacks that I think you might enjoy.

Take good care of yourself.

Best wishes,

Valerie

Letters of condolence

Death is said to be the last great taboo in Western society – we are not very good at dealing with it, though things do now seem to be improving gradually. Partly because of this collective inhibition about the whole subject, even those people who are most practised in the art of letter writing find letters of condolence amongst the most difficult to write. Many people shrink from the task for fear of intruding on the bereaved person's grief. The curious irony of this is that a grieving person's sense of loss and loneliness may be increased by the reserve or awkwardness of friends and acquaintances: being expected 'to get on with it' can prolong the grieving process, rather than shorten it. Sympathy and offers of support are comforting at any time of crisis or setback, but can be especially so when we have lost someone close to us. So try to put aside any fears you may have about doing 'the wrong thing' or 'finding the right words'. A simple and spontaneous acknowledgement of the loss suffered will almost always be appreciated and be of positive help to those most closely involved.

Many people opt to send a card with a short personal message written inside. However, do take care with your choice of card. Pre-printed messages can seem a little impersonal and it is often better to avoid those that include stock phrases or overly-sentimental clichés. Better still, make the effort to write a proper letter.

The following points may help to guide you, especially if you have not had to write such a letter before.

- A letter or message of condolence should, if possible, be handwritten.
- Formal letters of condolence to, for example, a business acquaintance, should always address the recipient by name.
- Try to use straightforward everyday words and phrases. It is probably best to avoid high-flown or flowery language and euphemistic expressions for death. Try not to use phrases like 'a blessed release' or 'a good innings'. Be sensitive to the feelings of the person who will read the letter.
- Only refer to God or prayer if you know that the recipient of the letter shares your belief.

To a business acquaintance (formal style)

405 Baird Drive
HOUSTON
Texas 0521

September 23 1999

Dear Mr Grosvenor

It was with deep sadness that I read of the sudden death of your business partner, Paul Cooper.

He will be greatly missed by the many clients who benefited from his wise counsel over the years, and will be long remembered for his unstinting efforts on their behalf.

My staff join me in sending our sincere condolences and deepest sympathy to you and members of his family.

Yours sincerely

Arthur Jenkins
Jenkins and Paterson

To a personal acquaintance (formal style)

67 Hatchgate Way
Lower Wheeling
Kent
DO12 4LT

19 October 1999

Dear Mrs Halliway

My sister and I were very sad to hear of your husband's death last Tuesday, and I write to offer sincere condolences to you and your family.

I am sure you know how much Mr Halliway was liked and respected in the village. We will all miss him greatly.

If there is anything we can do to help, please do not hesitate to get in touch.

Kindest regards

Margaret and Emily Chalmers

To a friend or relative (informal style)

16 West Park Avenue
CAMBRIDGE
Mass. 0539

February 3 1999

My dear David,

We were terribly sad to hear the tragic news of Barbara's death. It was a great shock, and we wanted you and the boys to know just how much you are all in our thoughts.

Barbara was loved by everyone who knew her, and we will treasure the memory of her warmth and kindness always.

You know that you can call on us at any time, and please don't hesitate if there is anything at all that we can do to help.

All our love

Tom and Anne

Letter informing someone of a death

4 Didsbury Hill
Didsbury
MANCHESTER
M11 4KS

4 April 1999

Dear Mr Knight

I am very sorry to have to let you know that my father, John Murray, died in hospital on Monday.

As you may know, he had been ill for some time. He fought very bravely and it was only in the final few days that his condition deteriorated so much that he had to be admitted to hospital. He died peacefully in his sleep.

I know you and my father had been friends for many years, and he often talked with affection of the fishing trips you used to make together.

The funeral service is at 1.30 p.m. on Friday 26th April at Minton Parish Church. We would be very pleased if you were also able to join us at my mother's house afterwards.

Yours sincerely

Brenda Murray

15

Electronic mail (e-mail) and fax

E-mail

Electronic mail (usually shortened to e-mail or email) is an alternative to post, telephone or fax available to those organizations and individuals that have access to the Internet, the world-wide network of computers interconnected through a mix of private and public telephone lines. E-mail is the most widely used function of the Internet with hundreds of millions of messages sent and received daily all over the world, and the volume of traffic is growing rapidly year by year. Its great appeal lies in its ease of use – no need for stationery, postage stamps, or trips to the post office. Every e-mail sent, no matter where in the world its destination, is charged at the rate of a local telephone call, and, unlike phone calls, you can keep copies of messages sent and received. Many people find e-mail so convenient that it prompts them to communicate much more than they would otherwise have done. However, as with all new toys, the novelty can soon wear off, especially if you receive loads of junk e-mail or if people bombard you with trivial messages on a daily basis.

How to get connected

You can get on-line (connect to the Internet) in one of several ways: by dial-up connection, ISDN (Integrated Services Digital Network), or leased line. Dial-up connection is currently the commonest way of connecting a home computer to the Internet. You will need a modem to connect your PC or Apple Mac® to the telephone line (these are nowadays routinely packaged with new computers), and an e-mail program must be loaded to your machine. Next you need to choose an ISP or Internet service provider (also known as an IAP or Internet access provider), a company that operates one of the large computers (servers) that form one of the links that make up the Net and act as a sort of temporary mail box, storing your electronic mail until you are ready to receive it. Shop around before selecting an ISP; certain companies offer free access, and some high-street computer retailers offer free Internet access as an incentive to customers to buy their hardware. Once you have signed up with a service provider, you will get an e-mail address or addresses, and the provider will give you step-by-step advice on the information required to configure your modem so that it automatically dials their telephone number when you want to connect to the Net.

E-mail addresses are made up of two parts, like this: *bennie@fastdeal.co.uk*. The first part of the name (before the @ symbol) is the user name (ie your name or any nickname you choose to be known by); the second (after the @ symbol) is the domain name or host name (ie the server through which your mail is sent and received). The domain name is made up of subdomain, followed by domain type (the type of organization), followed by a country code (this last is omitted for many of the large host names based in the United States, like AOL® and Compuserve®). The elements in the domain name are separated by dots.

ⓘ It is important to type the exact address – get a single character wrong and the e-mail will not get through. Note also the address should be typed with no spaces between characters and no full stop at the end.

Sending an e-mail

When you want to send an e-mail, select the e-mail software's icon or file menu option for creating a new message. A window will open made up of a series of boxes into which you type the destination address (or addresses), a heading or subject, and the text of your message.

Here we've used the 'New Message' window from the Eudora Light® e-mailing program to show the general layout – all the newer programs have the same or similar features, including an address book for storing the names and e-mail addresses of people you contact regularly.

staff@publigraph.co, 16:39 15/03/99, Computer Training: DTP

Standard | MIME | QP | Send

To: staff@publigraph.com
From: Andrew Gormley <agormley@publigraph.com>
Subject: Computer Training: DTP
Cc:
Bcc:
Attached:

Training sessions in DTP run by CompuDirect are being arranged for Tues 8, Wed 9, and Thur 10 June in the Training Centre (Room 47A).

Can you let me know the name of any staff member from your dept who has not attended previous CompuDirect courses and who will be available to attend these sessions? Each session is, as before, from 10.30 a.m. to 3.30 p.m. with an hour's break for lunch.

Thanks

Andrew Gormley
Trng Mngr

If you type more than one destination address in the first box, the addresses should be separated either by a comma or a semicolon, depending on the software program being used. If you are using an address book, you can select multiple recipients in the To: box, the Cc: box , and the Bcc: box, simply by clicking on each name in turn.

The Cc: (carbon copy) box and Bcc: (blind carbon copy) boxes are used for sending copies of the message. The blind copy box is used to send a copy of the message to someone whose name you do not want to be shown on the message received by those named in the To: and Cc: boxes.

Include a subject or heading in the appropriate box – this will help both you and the recipient(s) to file the message so that it is easier to find and refer to later.

It isn't strictly necessary to use a complimentary opening in e-mail, though many people prefer to start their messages with a greeting of some sort. Where a greeting is used it is often more conversational in style than the conventional 'Dear ...,'.

It is also possible to add a 'signature' automatically to each e-mail you send. Your signature might include such details as your name, title, company name, address, telephone number and fax number. To create a signature click on your e-mail package's Tools menu and the Mail Format option, or its equivalent.

E-mails are usually sent in plain text. Plain text has no formatting, like this:

```
The quick brown fox jumped over the lazy dog.
```

Some newer e-mail programs also allow you to send messages in HTML format and/or Rich Text format. HTML (Hypertext Markup Language) is used to create Web pages on the World Wide Web and offers the variety of type faces and sizes normally only available in word-processing programs; bold, italic and underlining; bullets and numbering in various styles; alignment and horizontal lines; and background styles. The Rich Text format has text formatting options, bullets and alignment. However, even if your e-mail program offers the options of HTML format and Rich Text format, you should always use plain text unless you are sure that the recipient of your message also has them as part of their software.

Another great advantage of using e-mail is that it allows you to attach graphics, word-processed, spreadsheet and even program files to the message and send them through cyberspace with your message. This means that there is no need to print out or load these files onto disk/CD-ROM and send them separately through the conventional postal system. Again, you should first check with the person to whom you are sending an attached file that they have appropriate software that will allow them to open and read the attachment. If you receive e-mail with attachments, there is a risk that an attachment may contain a computer virus. Attached files should only be saved to your hard disk if you trust the person sending it and/or you run a virus check on the file attachment before saving.

If you want to reply to a message received, there is no need to create a new message. Just click on the Reply icon and type your return message in the space that appears above the original. The reply will be sent automatically to the original sender and a copy of their message together with your reply is thus kept together under the same subject heading.

E-mail etiquette

Because e-mail is a new medium for rapid communication, the writing style is generally informal, making frequent use of abbreviations and acronyms. This informality, and the tendency to use shortened forms, cause some problems. It is worth putting a little thought into the composition of your message, especially if it is being sent in plain text format. While you may intend it to be read in a particular way, this may not always come over. Use only abbreviations and acronyms that you are confident the person you are messaging will understand. Avoid sarcasm and irony unless the recipient is familiar with your style. Also, do not make defamatory, libellous or offensive comments about people, groups or organizations in e-mail messages: you may find yourself on the wrong end of a lawsuit.

The early users of e-mail developed various methods for conveying emotion in their messages. For example, typing entire words or strings of words in capital letters is the written equivalent of shouting, and should therefore be used with caution, or not at all.

A coding system also evolved to represent various emotions, such as happiness, sadness, etc. The combination of characters used to represent a particular emotion is known as an emoticon. Many emoticons are made up of combinations of keyboard characters that create faces when viewed sideways on – these are known as smileys. Here are some examples:

:-) = happy
:- (= sad
;-) = winking
:-O = shocked
):-| = frowning

The use of emoticons is only really appropriate in personal messages or those exchanged by like-minded people in a newsgroup.

As has already been mentioned, abbreviations and contractions are very common in e-mail. New ones appear daily, but here are some examples that you might come across:

AFAICT = as far as I can tell
AFAIK = as far as I know
AFK = away from keyboard

AIUI = as I understand it
B4 = before
BAK = back at keyboard
BBL = be back later
BTW = by the way
cld = could
doc = document
EOF = end of file
FAQ = frequently asked question
FOC = free of charge
foll = following or to follow
FWIW = for what it's worth
FYI = for your information
GR8 = great
HTH = hope this helps
IIRC = if I recall correctly
IMHO = in my humble opinion
IMO = in my opinion
IOW = in other words
ISTM = it seems to me
ITRO = in the region of
NRN = no reply necessary
NW! = No way! or No!
msg = message
OTOH = on the other hand
OTT = over the top
PD = public domain
prhps = perhaps
TBD = to be discussed
TIA = Thanks in advance
TNX = Thanks
TVM = Thanks very much
VR = virtual reality
WRT = with regard to

Security

Up-to-date software programs have begun to tackle the question of e-mail security. E-mails can be encrypted so that they cannot be read by anyone other than the recipient. The use of a digital signature or 'digital ID' means that you can check that the person sending an e-mail to you is who they say they are. Some of the latest word-processing and spreadsheet programs allow you to protect files using passwords so that the file is secure when you send it over the Internet attached to an e-mail. Each of these security measures requires that both you and the recipient have compatible software and/or knowledge of the password used.

Fax (facsimile)

Fax is another quick and convenient way of sending documents (both handwritten and printed) using telephone lines. Faxes are sent and received using a special machine which photographs the document and converts this image into digital form for transmission via the telephone network to another fax machine, which then prints it out.

Fax is widely used in business and is useful for sending messages and documents that for one reason or another must reach their destination quickly, but cannot be sent via the Internet. However, scanners linked to computers can convert documents into computer files which may then be sent via the Internet, and it is likely that fax machines will decrease in popularity as computer technology advances and becomes more affordable. Many personal computers now include a facility for fax, and this has an added advantage in that you can read the fax and store it on your computer hard disk, without ever having to print it out.

A faxed document should always be accompanied by a cover sheet that includes details of the sender, how many pages are being sent, and who the message is intended for.

As with e-mail, the language of fax messages tends to be more informal, and it is not necessary to include a greeting line or complimentary close.

16

Word-processing

Word processors have all but replaced typewriters in both office and home. As each year passes, new features are added to the popular word-processing software packages, making them relatively easy to use – with a little practice. In the future, it is likely that more of us will bypass the keyboard altogether and dictate directly to our personal computers using voice recognition software. Meanwhile, word-processing programs enable even those of us who are 'two-finger' typists to produce professional-looking letters relatively quickly and easily. With a word processor, text can be moved around, edited, formatted, and checked for spelling and grammar errors. If you are going to use your personal computer to create letters, you will also have to own or have access to a printer. But, word-processing on a computer does away with the need for carbon copies – the letter can be saved to your hard disk, or an extra copy printed for your files.

Computers/word-processors are a positive boon for the blind and partially-sighted or anyone who has difficulty writing by hand. Predictive software can save the disabled typist time by guessing what the word being typed is, saving on the keystrokes that would usually be required to complete it.

Word-processors often come as part of the software 'suite' supplied with new personal computers. The software can also be bought separately in computer shops or by mail order. Computer magazines are a good source of advice. They often have articles or special sections comparing the merits of the products available on the market.

Spelling and grammar checking

Most word processors have some sort of spell checking facility, which will operate as you type or will search the completed document for any spelling errors.

Spell checkers use dictionary databases, and their efficiency is therefore dependent on the number and range of words included in the dictionary. Spell checkers may only recognize a limited number of proper names, or they may be stumped by technical or scientific terms.

ⓘ A word of caution: it is still worth re-reading your letter after the spell check has been done. If you have used the wrong word, but have spelt it correctly, the spell checker will not pick it up. Particular care should be taken with words whose spellings are frequently confused, like *practise* and *practice*, *affect* and *effect*, *dependant* and *dependent*.

Your word processor may also include a grammar checker, which will identify errors in grammar and usage.

Some word-processing programs allow you to customize the spelling and grammar check to suit the style of language used in the document, eg standard, informal, formal or technical.

Help with vocabulary and content

Other useful features that may come with your word processor are a thesaurus and a summarizing tool (which will highlight the main points in your letter and help in paragraphing).

Office software packages

The 'office' software packages now widely available (and which have a word-processing program as part of the package) include some useful features that help in letter-writing:

Letter templates

You can choose one of the letter templates that come with the software package, or you can design your own, save it and use it for each new letter that you write.

Address book

The electronic address book is a useful feature that can be shared by the various applications in your computer: word-processor, e-mail program, etc. You need only type a person's details (name, job title, company name, postal address, e-mail address, fax number, telephone number) into the address book once. Thereafter, select a name in the address book using the mouse, and the computer will extract appropriate details for whichever means of communication you are using: name and address to be added to a letter, e-mail address for a new message, fax number for the fax cover page, or telephone number for automatic dialling.

Letter wizard

Wizards are short-cut features that bring together all the standard commands required to perform a series of tasks. As the name implies, the letter wizard will do much of the formatting of your letter 'by magic', as well as allowing you to add, with a couple of mouse clicks, certain specific elements, such as the date or a reference line. It can format an entire letter automatically and minimizes the number of keystrokes the writer has to make. You can also opt to structure your letter as you type using whichever letter style you have selected, eg blocked or indented, business letter, formal letter or informal letter. You can also select, from various menus offered by the wizard, the date, a salutation, and a complimentary closing.

Automatic formatting and correction

An alternative to the letter wizard is the automatic formatting command. By selecting this function in the Tools menu and choosing 'Letter' from the menu of document types, you are able to automatically format as you type, or when the typing is completed.

Automatic correction is used to correct typing errors as they are made, such as *teh* for *the* or *aslo* for *also*. It will also correct accidental use of capital letters and various other common typing errors.

Standard or form letters

If you regularly use standard letters to send to clients, customers or suppliers, this feature enables you to produce multiple copies of a letter (each with a different addressee and any other details that may be required to personalize it) without laboriously having to type a copy for each recipient. Form letters use the facility known as 'mail merge'. Mail merge makes use of data sources like mailing lists or your own computer address book. The machine will automatically insert into the form letter the relevant data from the mailing list, producing a personalized copy for each person or company on the list.